WHO AM I WITHOUT YOU

A Journey Through Loss, Grief, and Love

MIRELA LEMUT

Who Am I Without You

Copyright © 2025 by Mirela Lemut.

MILTON & HUGO L.L.C.
4407 Park Ave., Suite 5
Union City, NJ 07087, USA

Website: *www. miltonandhugo.com*
Hotline: *1- 888-778-0033*
Email: *info@miltonandhugo.com*

Ordering Information:
Quantity sales. Special discounts are granted to corporations, associations, and other organizations. For more information on these discounts, please reach out to the publisher using the contact information provided above.

Library of Congress Control Number: 2025921690
ISBN-13:   979-8-89285-668-3   [Paperback Edition]
                    979-8-89285-669-0   [Digital Edition]

Rev. date: 09/17/2025

To my parents who created a strong woman out of me, and my sister, who no matter the difficult road she travelled always remained happy. To all my bunnies who have brought joy back into my life after my family's passing. To my lost bunnies who inspired me to put my feelings onto paper and heal with it. To my daughter, Melinda, who is my greatest creation in life. My anchor, my life and my new beginning.

1

Heartbreak
Nothing but the endless what ifs
To my bad decisions
Nothing but the endless what ifs
That can never be taken back
Nothing but the endless what ifs
That will never bring you back.

2

My beautiful Elizabeth
There will never be another
Who can take my breath away
There will never be another
With such style and grace

3

I am so sick of this life
Nothing ever changes
You never change
You never learn
You never appreciate
You always stay the same
Watch me as I turn and walk away

4

I heard the scuffle
But failed to react
Blinded by my own agony
And you needed me
And I failed you
And I failed me

5

Elizabeth the Great
You were destined for greatness
As you were a Christmas miracle
You took away my daily stresses
As you showered me with kisses
You were our angel
As you ever were and never be again

6

I miss you
I miss me
I want to go back
And choose differently
I want to go back
And take you with me
I want to go back
And stay with you

7

So much pain
So much loss
I'm so lost
I'm stuck in time
Unable to move forward
I'm falling back into depression
But I need to find a way to move on

8

What is the point of this life
When all I feel is pain
What is the point of this life
When all my dearests keep disappearing

9

Brownie
My sweet little fur ball
Just as we started bonding
You chose to walk away
Now mommy is left heartbroken
Not knowing if you are dead
But yet knowing you are no longer here
My little Brownie
You were meant for so much more

10

In one moment
One stupid error in judgment
Changed both of our lives
Forever
My selfishness took away your life
You died so young and so wrong
There was so much more
That you could of done, lived
But my actions took that away
From you, from me
My heart is now broken
The guilt is eating at me
As it should be
While you were dying
I was hating on the moments
You were with me instead of another
Nothing but regret now in my heart
The words I can never take back
The words that never should of been spoken

11

I don't know how to go on
When every waking moment is with you
I don't know how to go on
When I'm no longer here without you
I hate her, I hate me
I hate the world
Where you can no longer be

12

I feel so broken, I miss you so much
My little man. My Mr. Peterson.
Where does one belong
When one belongs nowhere

13

Who am I?

I'm Mirela

What am I?

A mom, and a woman

What do I like to do?

Take care of my loved ones, my daughter, our bunnies

What are my hobbies?

Reading, writing, yoga, watching movies

What makes me happy?

?????

14

I want to go back to when life made sense
When I didn't regret waking up each day
knowing you're no longer there
I want to go back to life where I had dreams
and plans for my life
I want to go back to not feeling empty and
wasted
It has become so difficult living in this world
How did I get to this place of confusion and
sadness

15

I hate you
I hate me
I hate the world
For not taking me
Where you are
Is where I need to be

16

Forever lost
And no one is looking
What's my next step
Do I go left
Do I go right
Or do I keep drowning

17

Running away
Is like a single mother syndrome
Always on the run
Never feeling settled
When does it end
And when does it begin

18

What needs to happen
For things to change
Why is the simplest act of kindness
Turned into a nightmare.
A summer day with bright lights
And flowers, and splashing water
Is now a cold room, with darkness
And wasted explanations.
A summer day, a summer night
And an endless nightmare
Out of resources, out of guidance
How do you change the circumstances
When you don't know what the
Circumstance is.
And I continue to battle
This unseen force of nature
This beast with enormous
Strength and endurance.
In the end, was this even worth it
The question remains unanswered
Why was today different
Does it matter.

19

No one is a friend when you need one
Everyone here is to use you and nothing else
I have no one.
Friends are conveniently busy
And forgetful
When reaching out for help

Tab P11（2nd Gen）

20

Whatever happiness I had left in my heart
Died the night I found you lying dead on the
floor
Due to my ignorance you lost your life
This is something I can never forgive myself for
You were my precious little boy, my little man
I loved waking up next to you
And falling asleep knowing you were sleeping
by my side

21

I want to fly away
Fly away like a bird
Until my eyes get too weak to see
And my wings get too heavy to fly
Fly away to a better place
A place where the sun never ends
A happy place with my Lizzy, Tilly and my PB
I am ready, take me away
I want to be with my baby Lizzy, sweet Tilly
And my little man PB
There is nothing left for me here
My work is done
Take me away so this pain
Can finally end

22

Saying goodbye is never easy
Saying goodbye to the two of you is like a death
sentence
I wish that I can turn back the hands of time
And bring you both back to me
I hope that you both know just how much you
were loved
How much your lives changed mine for the
better
How angry and sad I am for the way things
ended
For my stupid mistakes that cost you both your
lives
Your presence in my life will greatly be missed
Forever in my heart your both will be
Forever in my heart is a great sadness due to
my stupidity
I lost you both
I will forever be incomplete as your lives meant
so much to me
The loss I felt after losing my parents and my
sister
The two of you filled
I will never be able to walk into my bedroom
and not want to cry
I loved you my little man

I am going to miss you more than you will ever
know
Please forgive me my sweet little PB, I am so
sorry for loosing you
I loved you so much, I thought that you were
lonely and needed a friend
I'm sorry that my actions cost you your life
I no longer have any happiness in my heart
Only tears and sadness my Mr. Peterson
:(:(

22

I am ready for the next chapter
My contract has been fulfilled
I want to go back to the water
My life is no longer here
I am ready to join you PB
My next chapter is with you

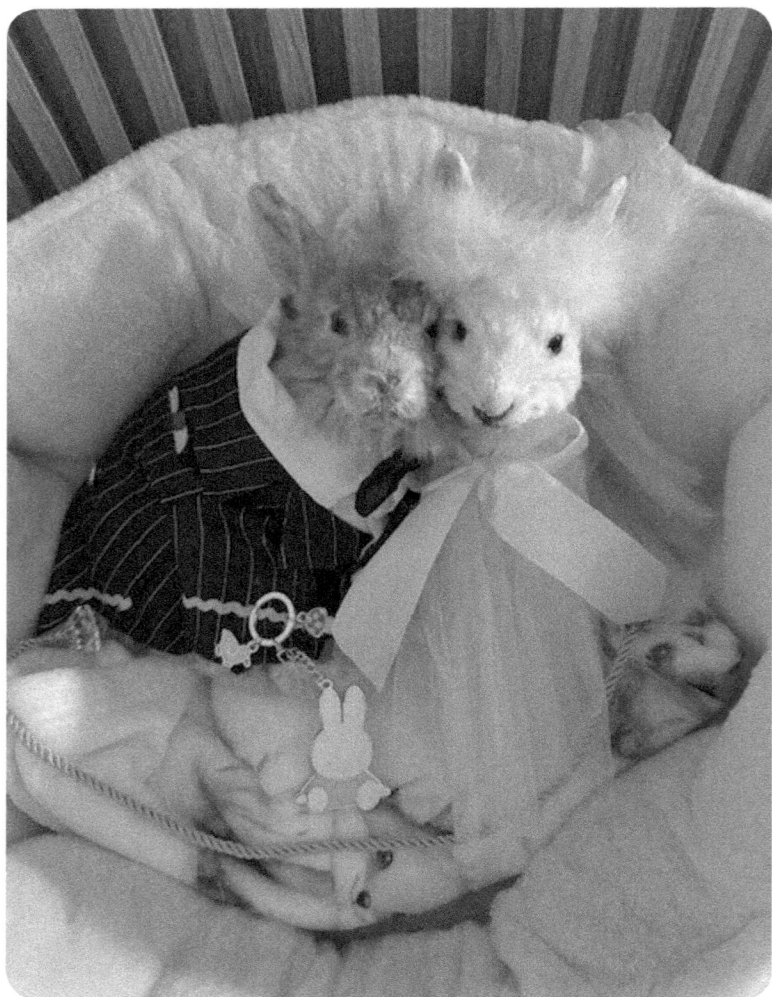

24

I'm drowning,
Someone please come save me,
What am I doing with my life,
Once four hearts beamed as one,
Now that only one is left, how does it go on.
Once a clear path in life,
And now, only sadness and confusion
Madness inside of me,
I want to fall asleep and not wake up.
I sit in silence,
Unable to move.
Telling myself that I need to get up,
But unable to move.
When life has lost all meaning.

25

I failed you my little Muffin
In the midst of my pain, I failed to see yours
My heart breaks for your loss
Muffin, you will never be forgotten
Dearest Muffin
The time we shared was brief
Though you impacted me for a lifetime
Until we meet again
Dearest Muffin
Forever in my heart you shall stay

26

Death shall have no dominion
One day our hearts will beat as one
Once again you and I will walk the same path
Dream of the same path
Once again feel love again together
My Vincent

27

What is a mother
I am a doorknob
I am a trash can
I am a maid
I am unworthy
I am annoying
I am a waste of space
I have nothing
I am nothing

28

Where does one belong
When one belongs nowhere
How does one go on
When one belongs nowhere
How the heart still beats
When it wishes to stay silent

29

Death follows wherever I go
Regardless of the paths I take
Death, like a faithful friend
Always waits patiently for me to arrive
No matter the distance
No matter the location
It follows me
It's followed me
To ensure that it breaks me
And it nearly did
Or maybe it did and
I just didn't know it
I am still here
Or are the footprints my imagination
I don't know anymore
As I no longer am the person in the mirror
I no longer am
As all that I am is hidden behind these tears
All that I am is where my heart longs to be
That is not here
Not anywhere near here
Not here, because you are no longer here
In my heart, yes you are
But not here in my arms
Where I can hold you
Not anywhere where I can feel you
Not anywhere where I need you to be

30

Death, like an old faithful friend
He leads, and I follow
Be wary of the words you speak
The last words
And the last thoughts.
I walked in through the front doors
You, lying on the floor
Staring into the nothingness
In this place of happiness
That is no more.
Lizzie, my princess
Her life cut short
By jealousy of others.
Others that are no longer here.
I spoke in anger of why instead of you
My Lizzie was not in my room
My princess, mi pequeña.
I screamed at the terror that lay in front of me
Confused in disbelief at what I was seeing.
I screamed and cursed myself
For what lay in front of me.
I threw myself on the floor and I grabbed you
You were still warm
But no longer with me
Oh my god
What have I done

My babies
What have I done
I hated what i said
I hated what I did
I hated the time
I hated the words
Words, that I can never take back.
I hated me
I hate me
I hate me
I hate me until the day I die.
Please forgive me my PB
Forgive the actions of a stupid mom
Who had to learn the hard way
Now my PB is no more
Mommy walks and breathes
But mommy no longer lives
I held you in my arms all night
Crying and begging god
To bring you back to me
But all he did was laugh
Laugh in my face
And take you away.
The last sparkle
That I had in my heart.
I have not suffered enough

He said, my faithful friend

Two years

7 souls

7 parts of me

That once were

My joy

My sadness

My fullness

I am no more

I am

And I am not

I live

But only to live

One day with

All of you

And no more

www.ingramcontent.com/pod-product-compliance
Lightning Source LLC
Chambersburg PA
CBHW032213040426
42449CB00005B/570